Happy Motivational Words
Adult Coloring Book

By Peaceful Mind Adult Coloring Books

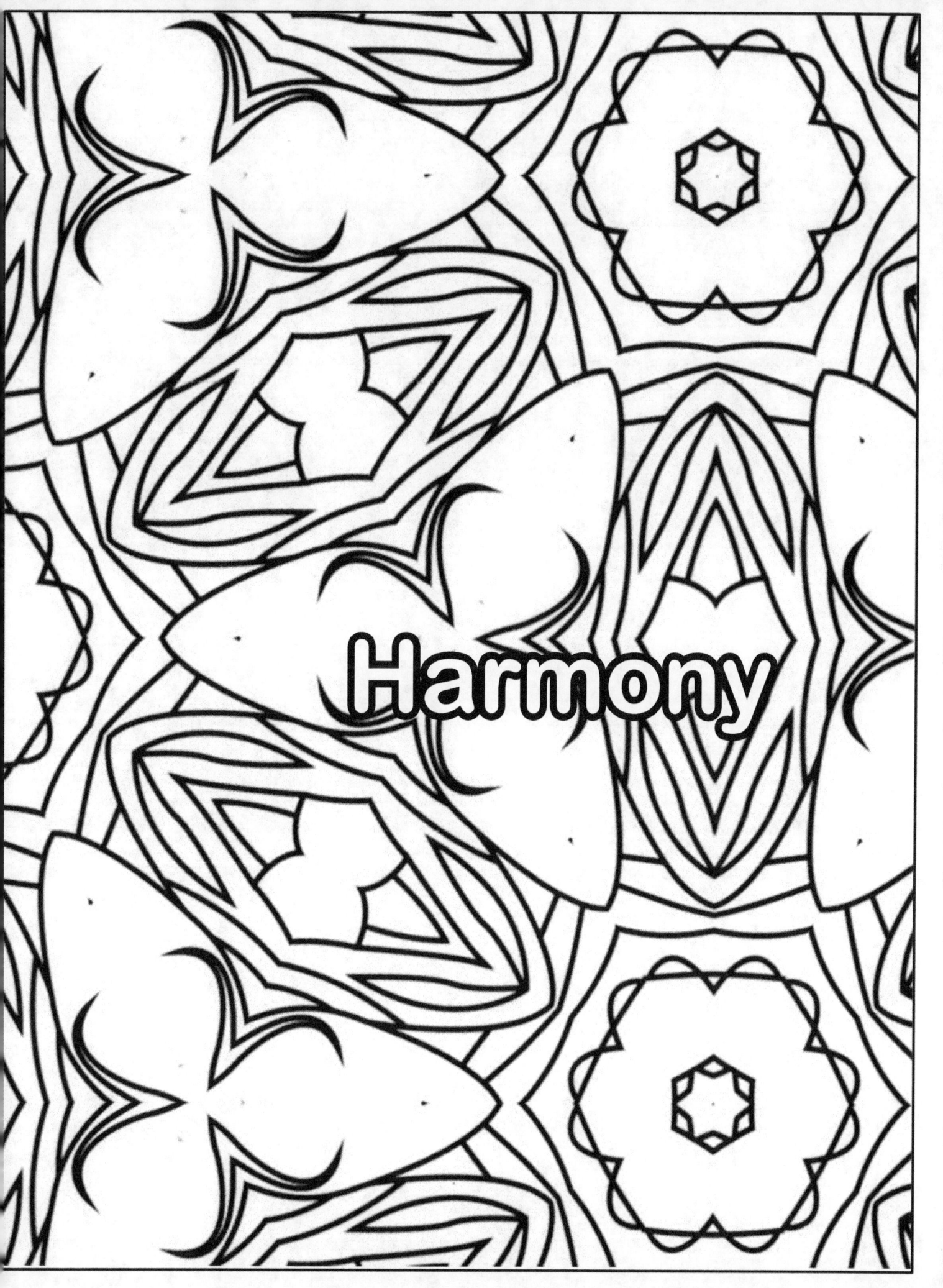

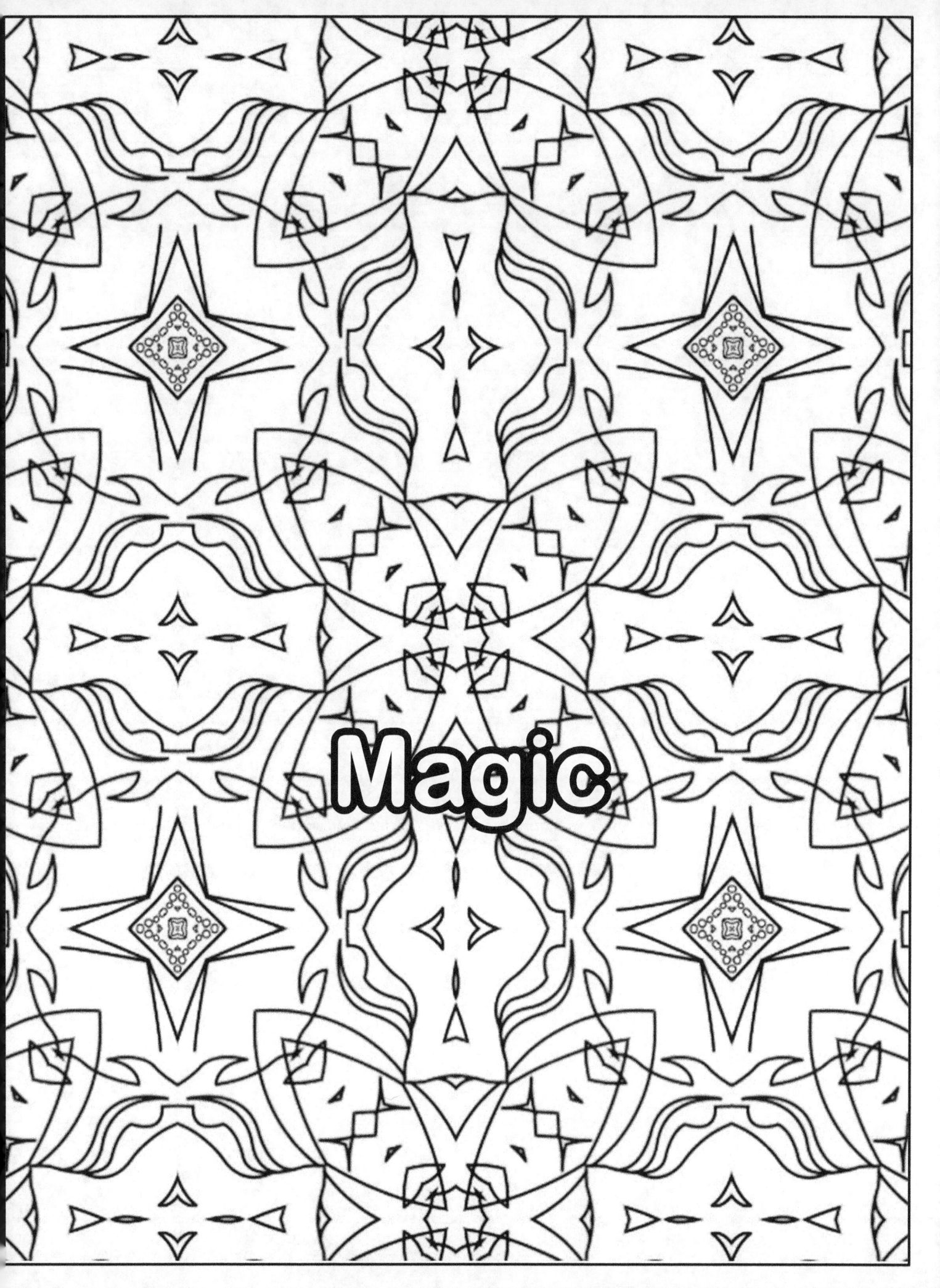

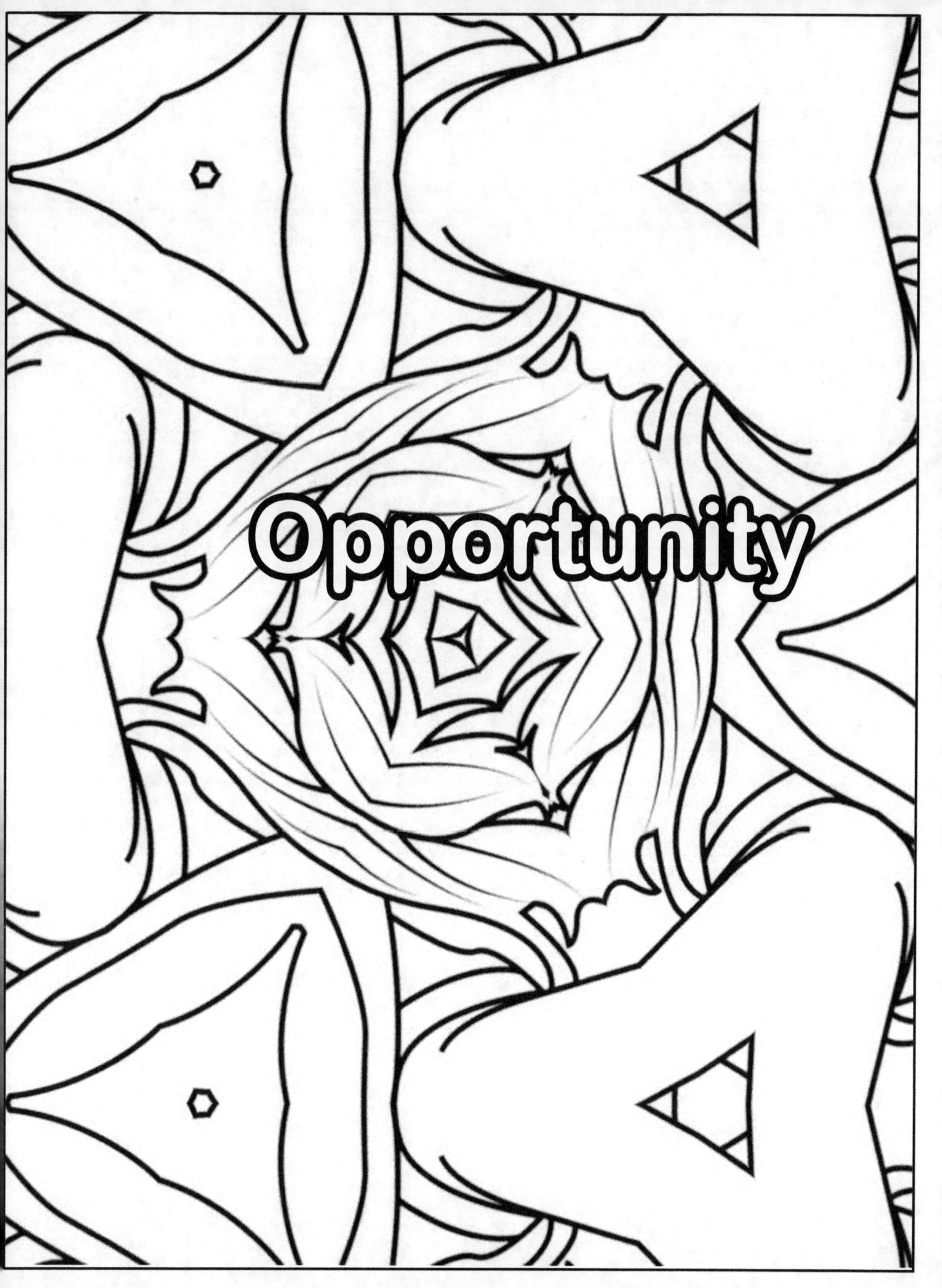

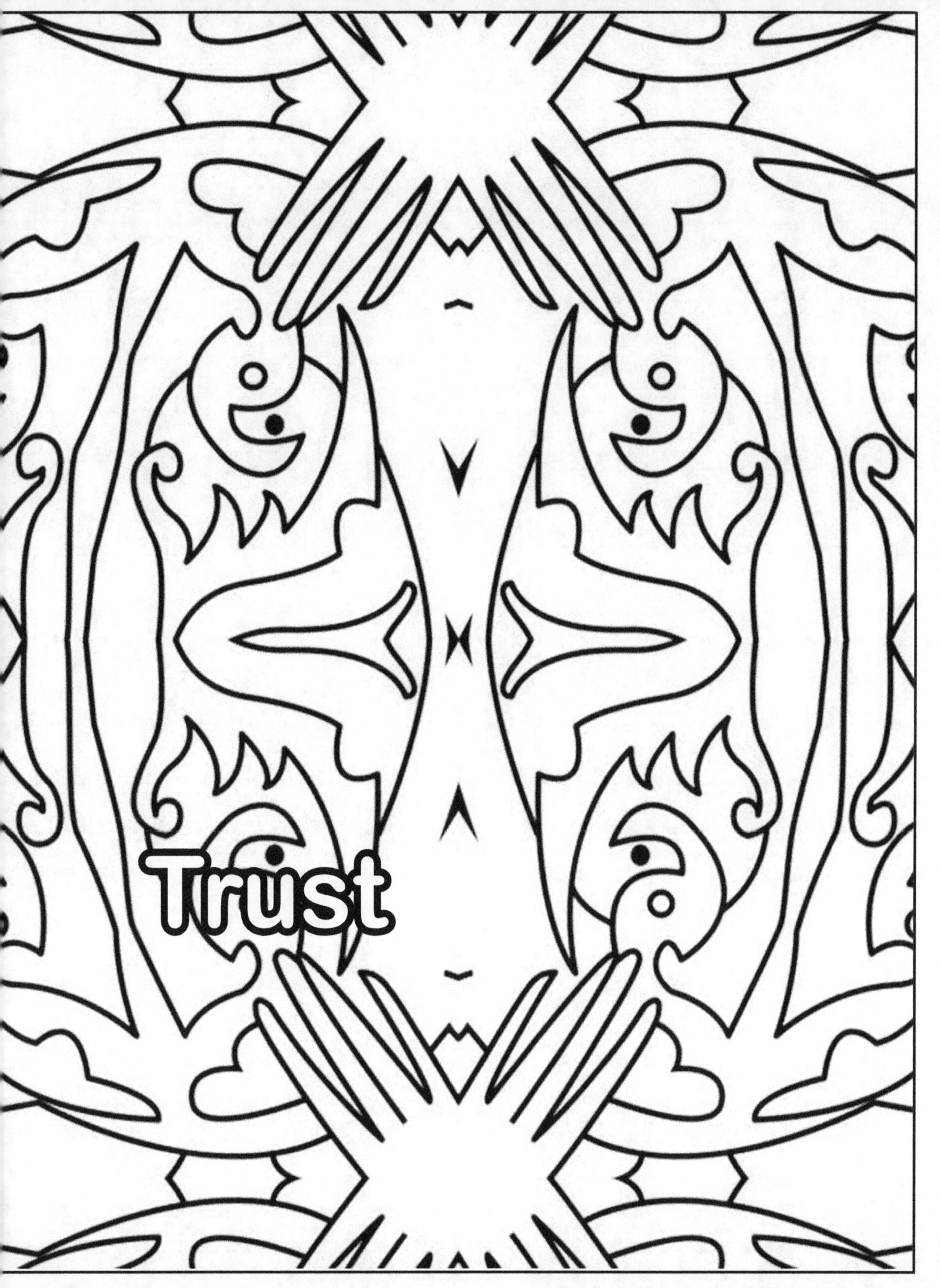

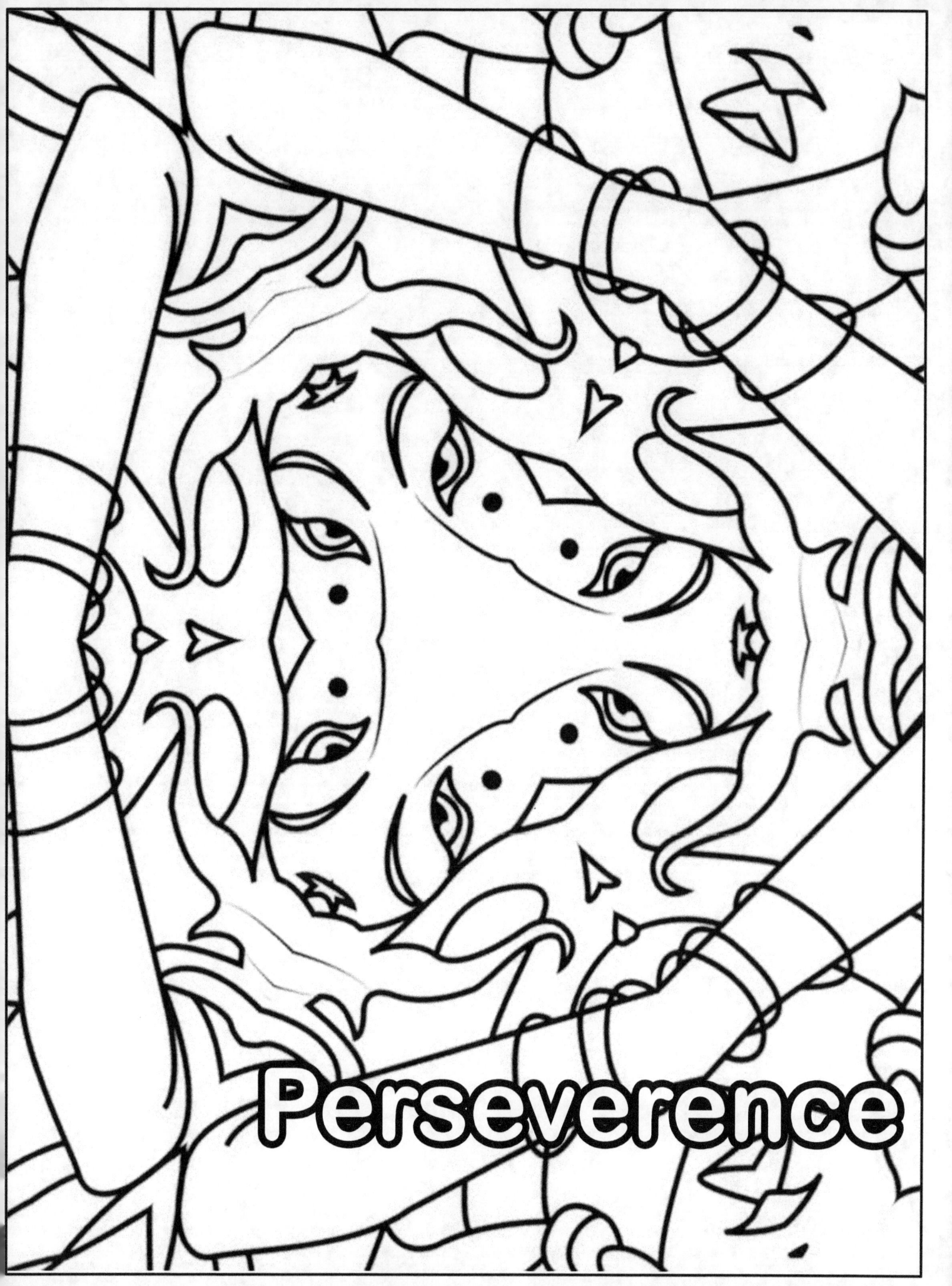

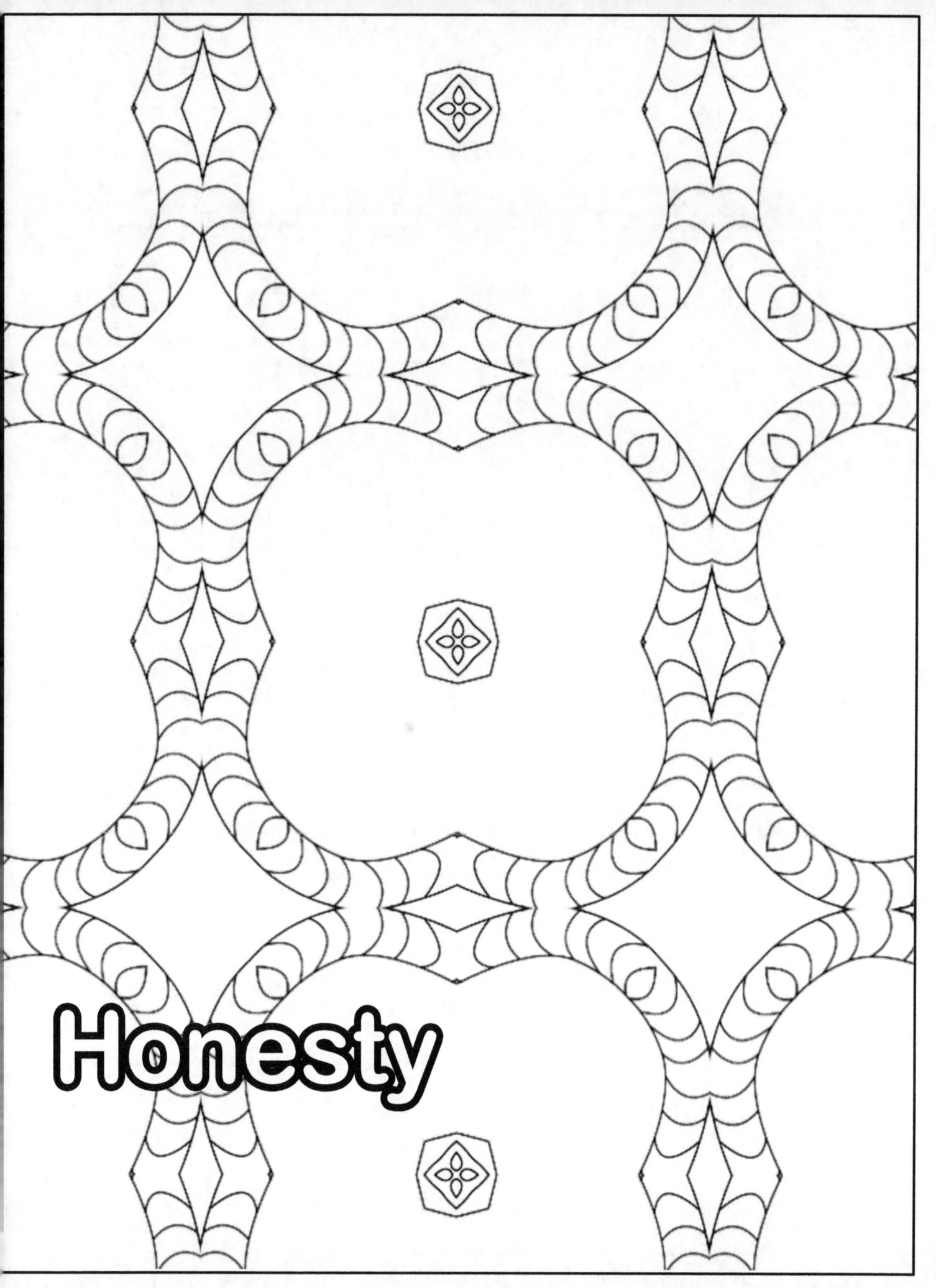

Honesty

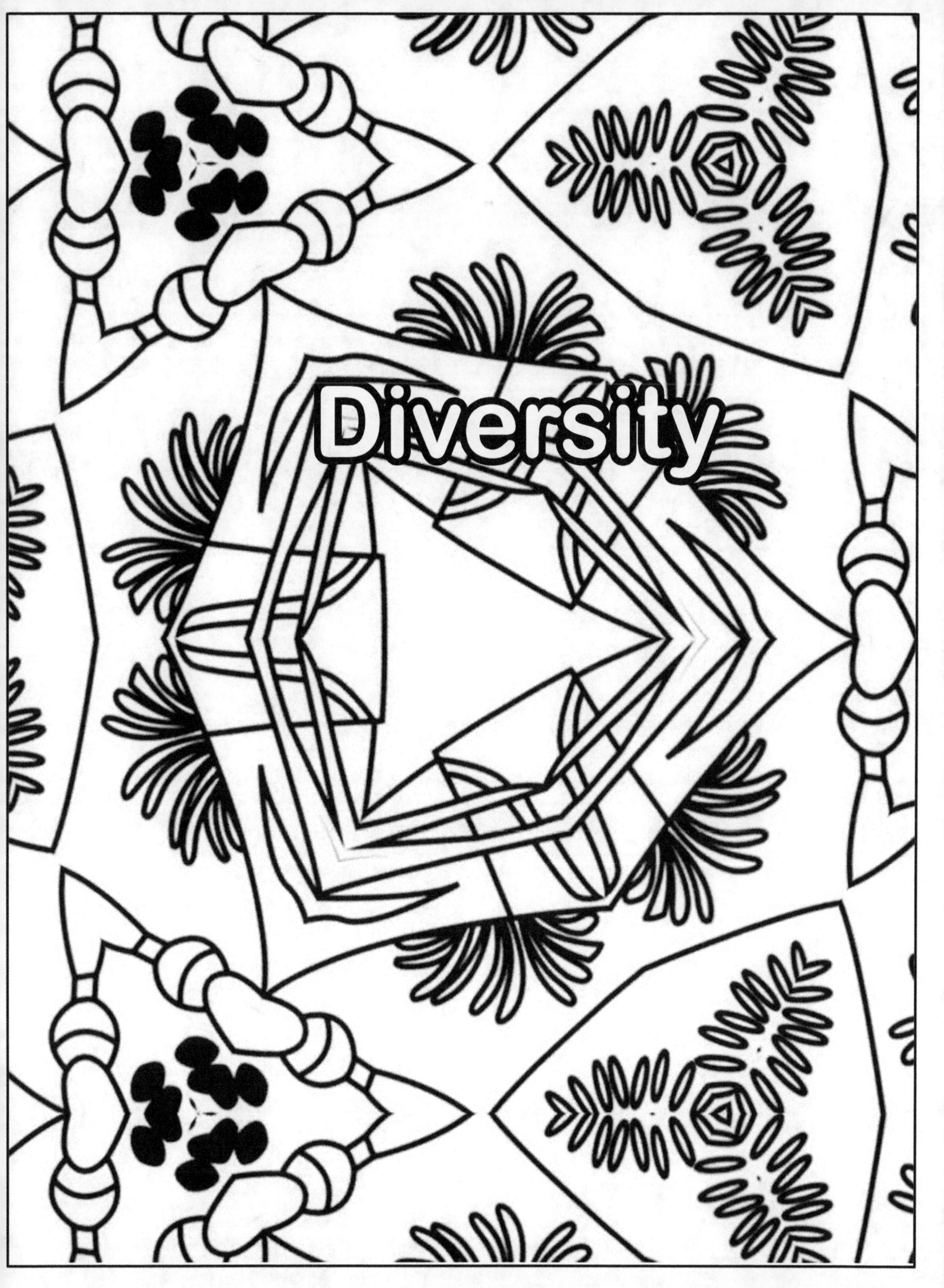

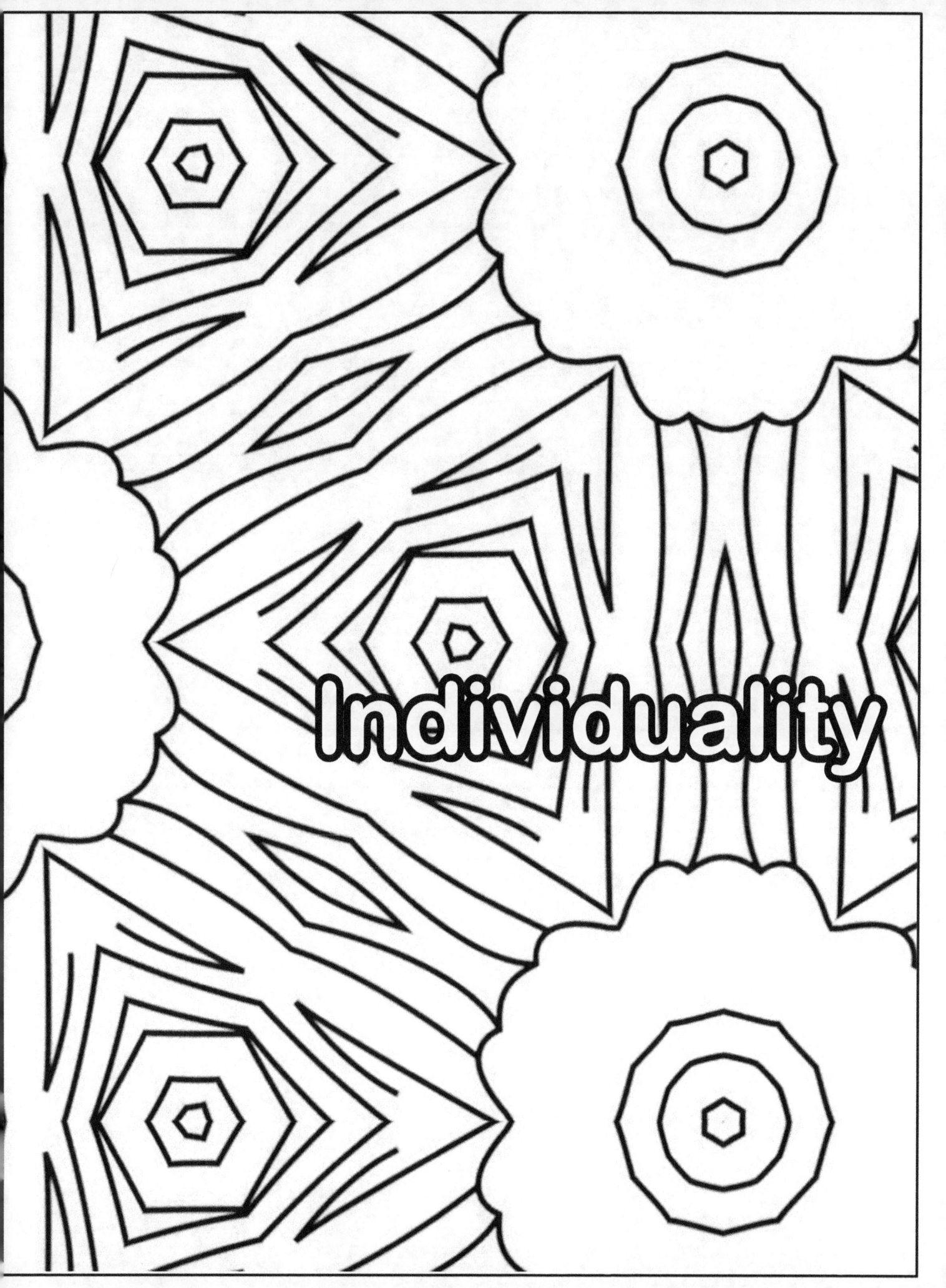

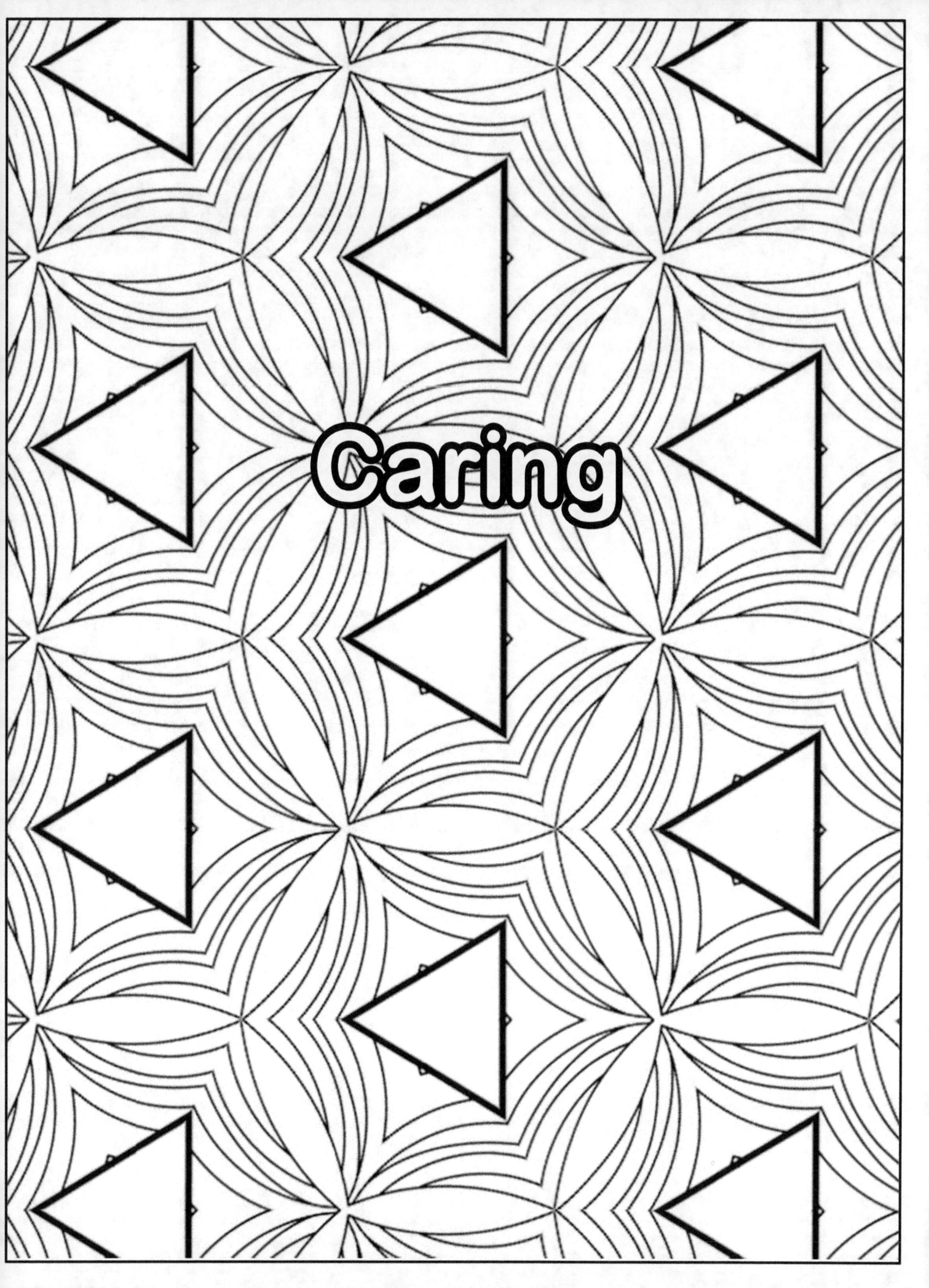

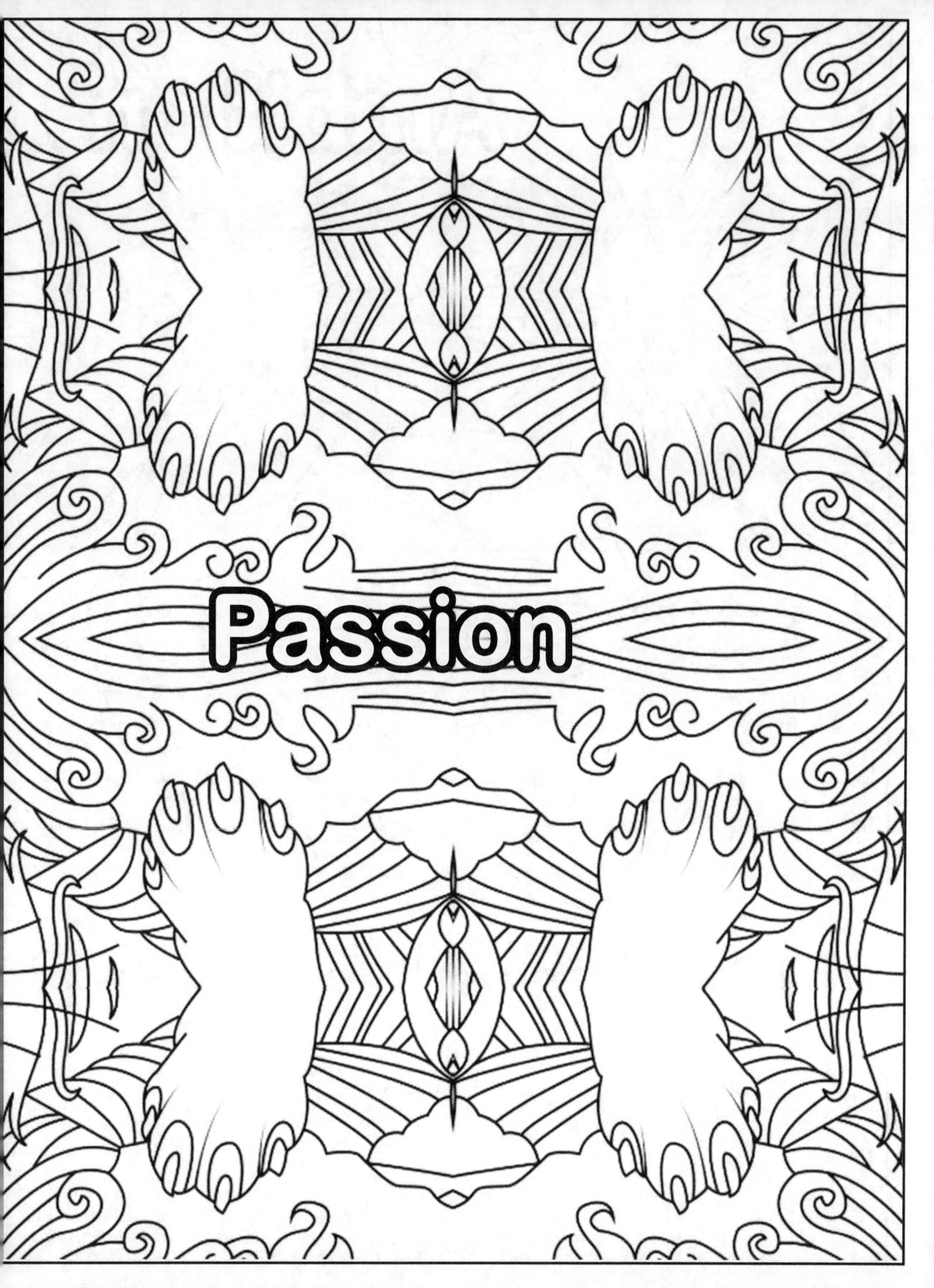

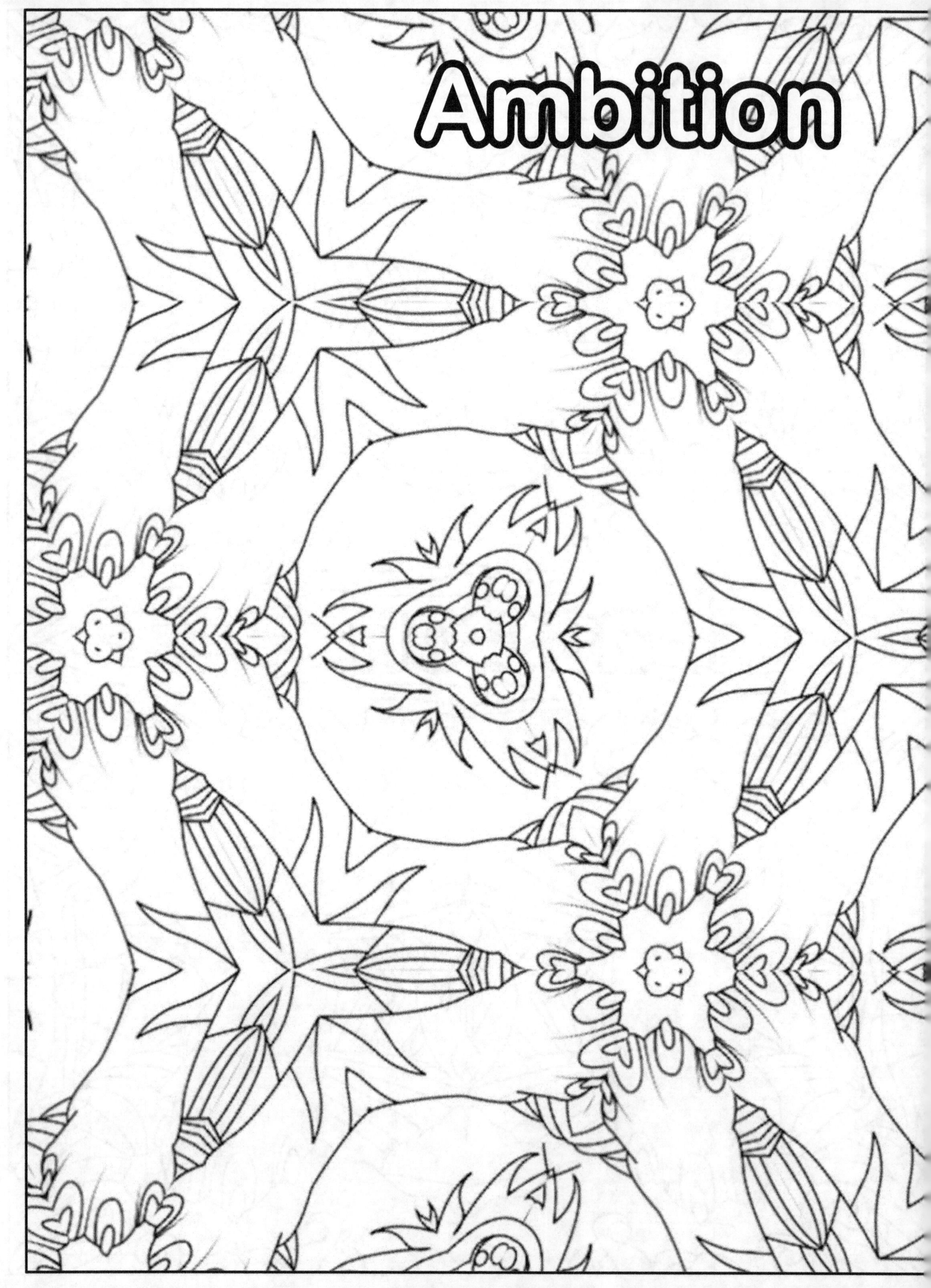

Ambition

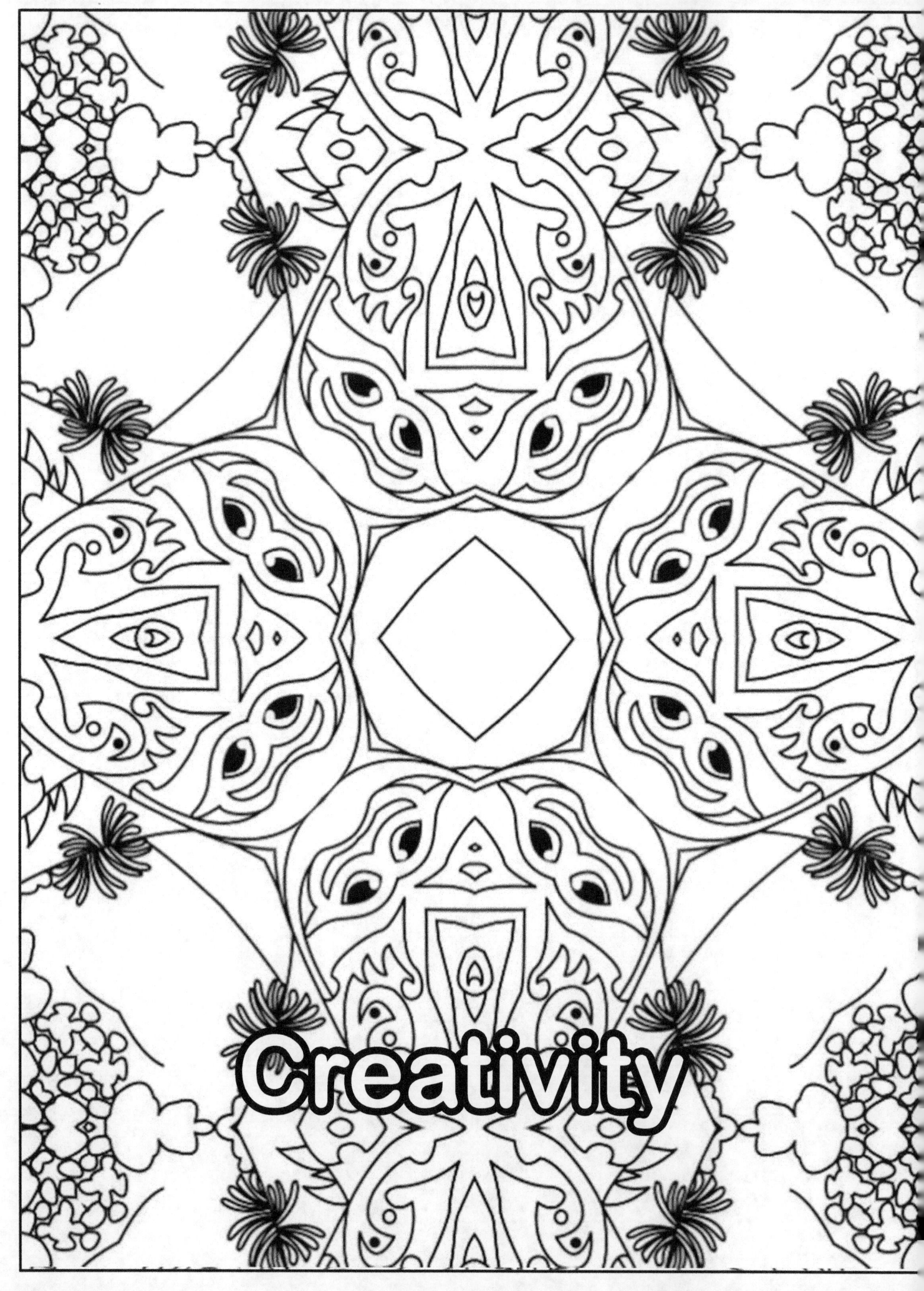
Creativity

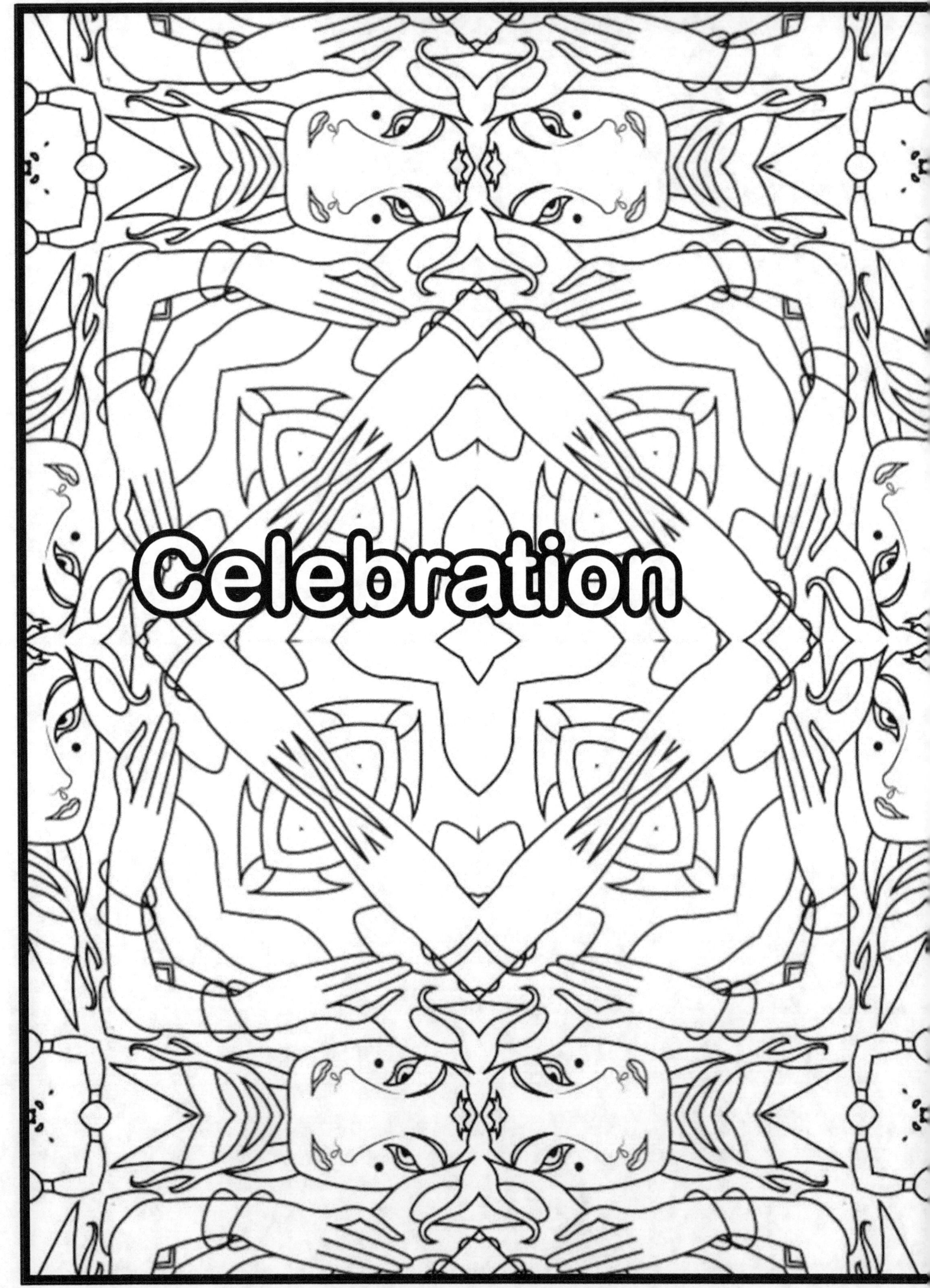

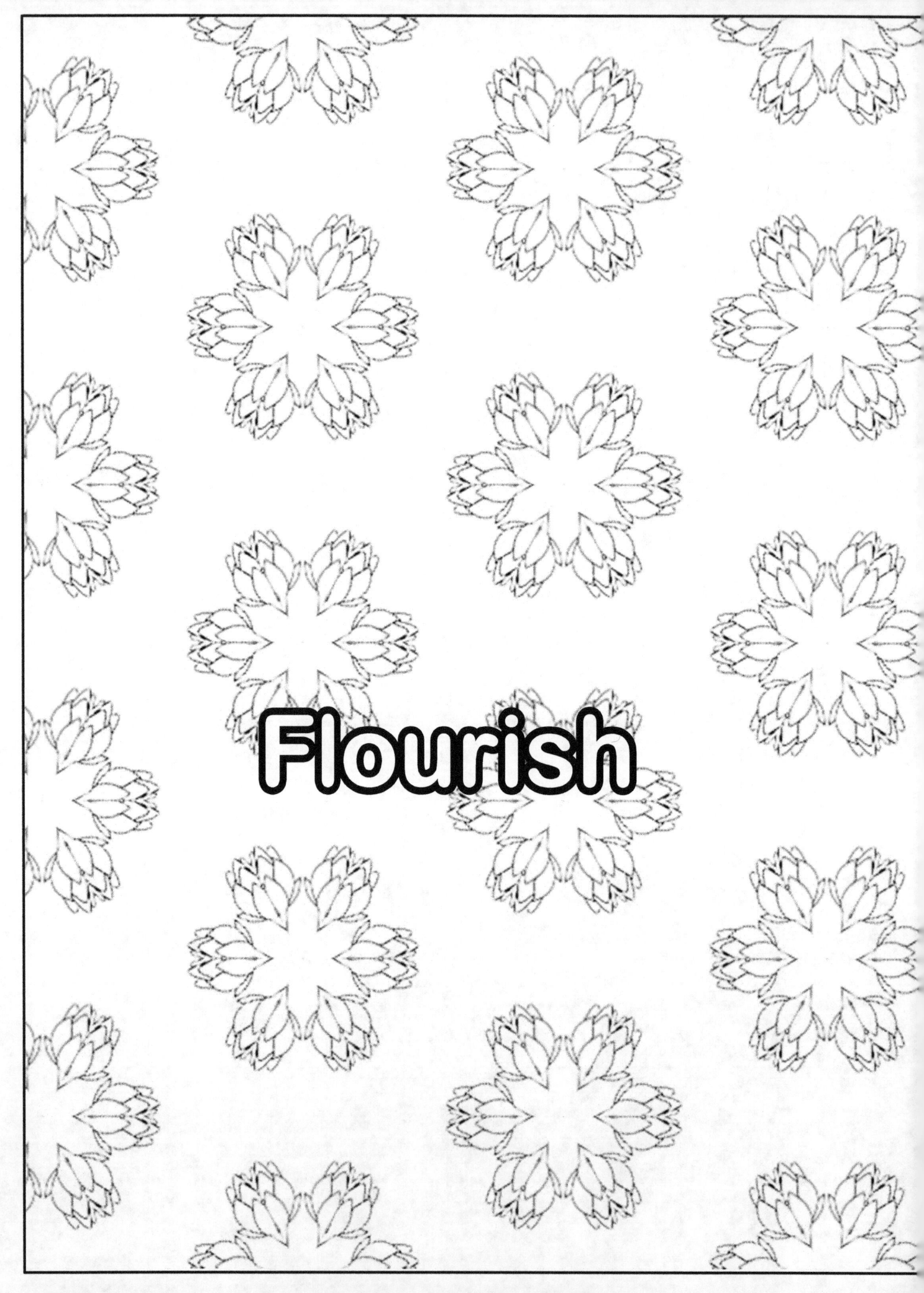

Flourish

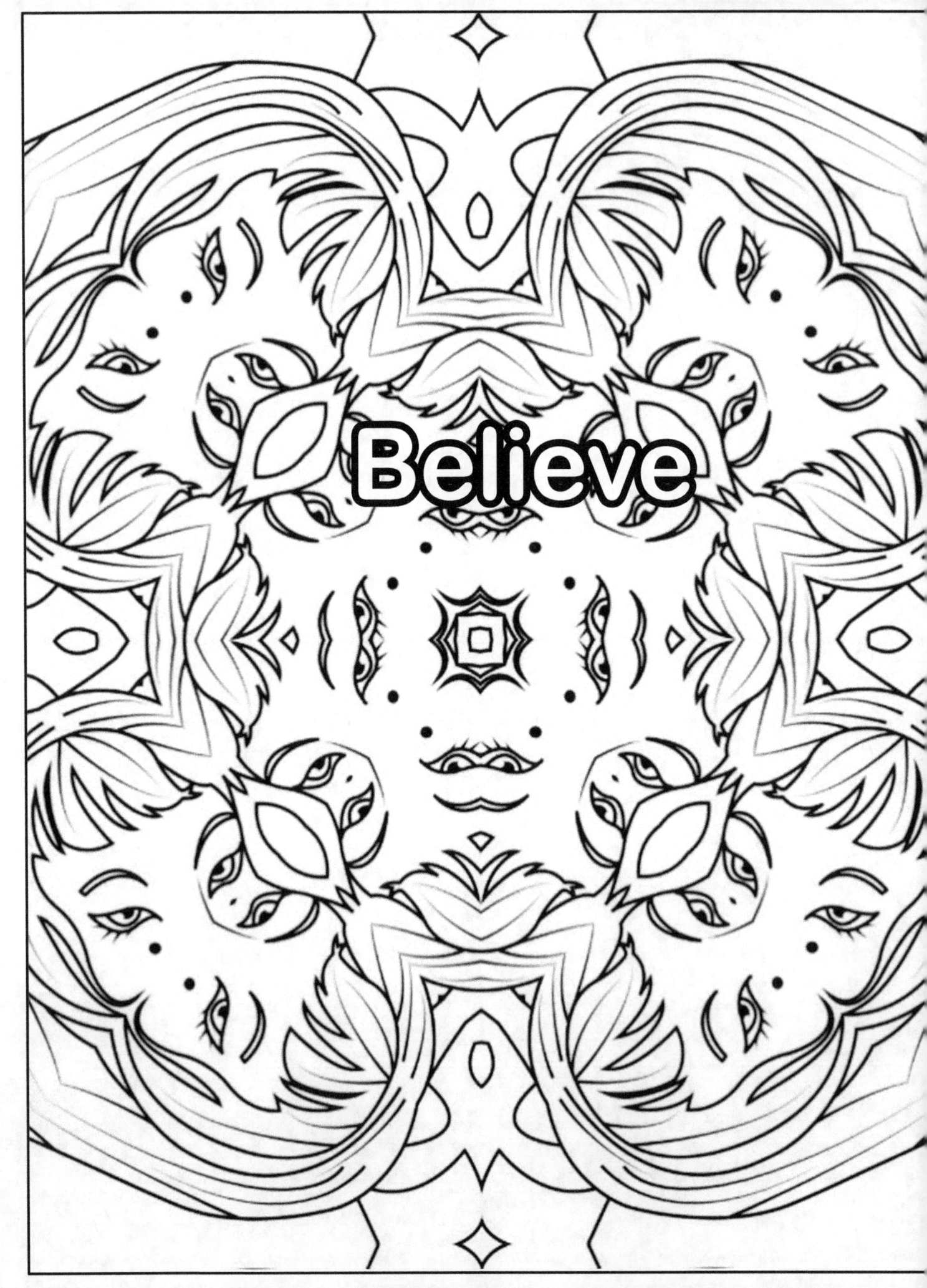

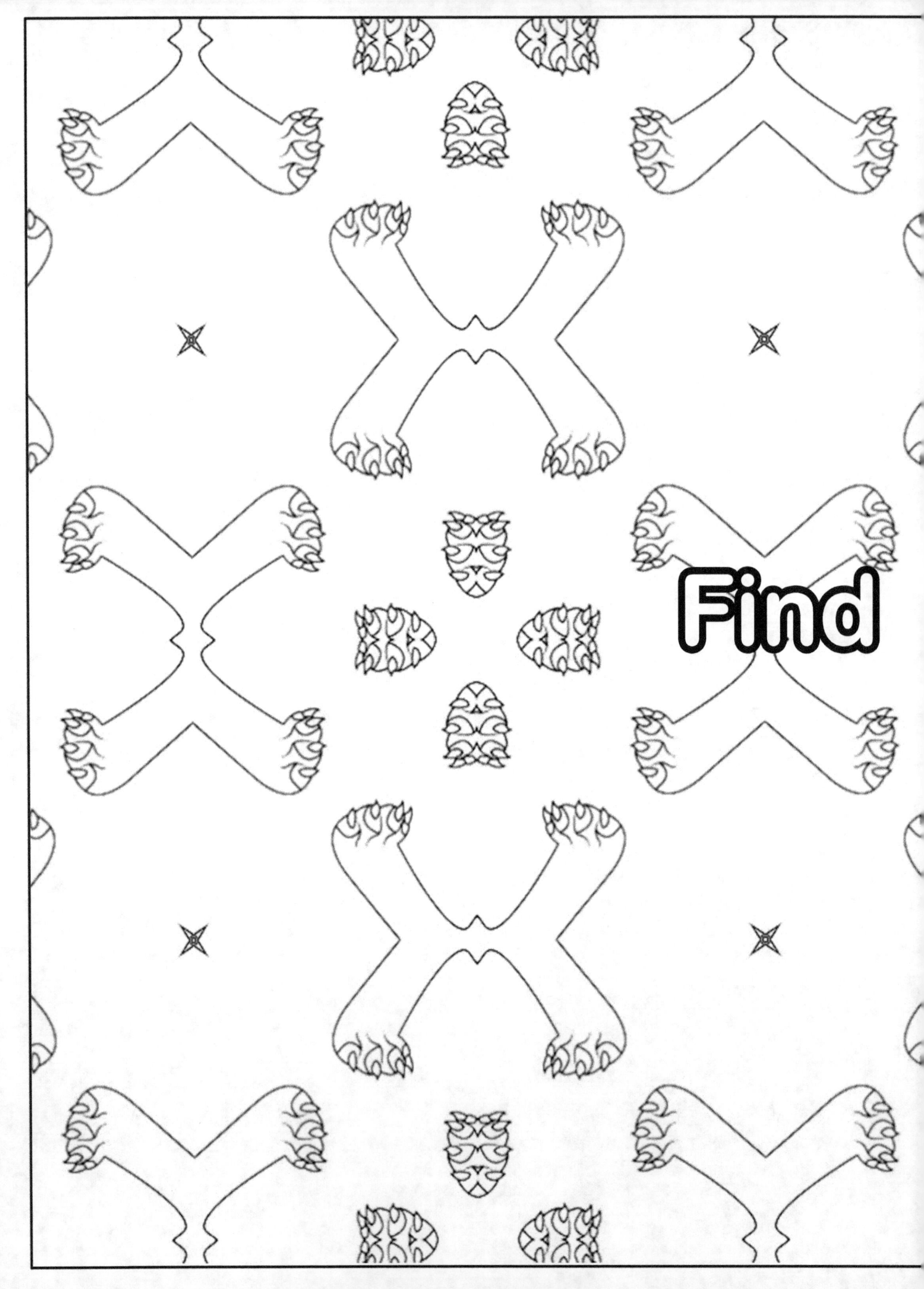

www.ingramcontent.com/pod-product-compliance
Lightning Source LLC
Chambersburg PA
CBHW080525190526
45169CB00008B/3054